I0085704

The Social Work *Hustle*™

The Social Worker's Guide to Making Money

How to navigate the highs, lows, and WTF moments in the world of Social Work

DHAIMA CHIN, LCSW

The Social Work Hustle™
Copyright 2019 Dhaima Chin, LCSW
All rights reserved.

This book or any portion thereof may not be reproduced or used in any manner whatsoever without the express written permission of the publisher except for the use of brief quotations in a book in review.

Cover Design & Interior Formatting by BrandItBeautifully.com

ISBN: 978-0-578-55311-5
Printed in the United States of America

DEDICATION

This book is dedicated to
you and your journey of becoming a Social Worker.

TABLE OF CONTENTS

ACKNOWLEDGMENTS

I would like to thank everyone for helping me on this pathway of success. In times of uncertainty, (and there will be many). May this book encourage and inspire you. I would like to express my profound gratitude to every member of my diverse tribe, you help me rise above every adversity.

Writing this book is a risk I'm willing to take.
Hopefully it's content will help and encourage thousands
more that I would not have been able to reach otherwise.

FOREWORD

I want to grow up and become a social worker because I know I can help the world and make a great living doing it said no one ever. We all were born with some dope gifts and developed a few passions and that tends to be the path we take unless life derails us, as it most always does.

We then choose paths on the pursuit of greater fulfillment. Changing people's lives and circumstances is one of the most mentally rewarding jobs and careers one can have, but why doesn't the pay match? I mean if we're doing some of the hardest and most vital work in the lives of our clients and making our agencies beaucoup cash why are we stuck in the hustle?

Many of us have contemplated changing majors, leaving the field and switching careers in order to make a living. Others work two or three jobs to keep a roof over their head and the lights on. We either make it through this thought process and time of struggle or we close the chapter on that story.

In this book, Author Dhaima Chin, not only speaks about what she was doing before the universe told her that she needed to make a shift, she also describes what the process was like in the making. Following her purpose wasn't the easiest thing to stick to as life knocked her down and kept swinging, but her determination took her to where she wanted to be as she continues to grow.

Dhaima is by far one of the sweetest, kind hearted, thoughtful and giving people that I have ever met. Our very first interaction took place on a cruise to Cuba for my first book launch, just a few days shy of one year ago. She was very quiet, reserved and literally stayed glued to the friend that she came with. As time went by, I saw her open up and soak in what was going on around her. She came home and hit the ground running to start her practice. She does so much for her community and has a passion for helping others, especially those who are social workers. A few months after we initially met, Dhaima aka Dee Dee, signed up to get a mentor through the Black Therapists Rocks Mentorship Program. As the Director of the program, I wanted to make sure she was matched with someone to suit what her goals were. She wanted to grow her practice, write a book and continue to help people pass their LCSW exam. I said to myself, "I can help her with that. Let me see if she wants to work with me or be assigned to someone else."

I then reached out to her and as I suspected, she agreed she would prefer me to be her mentor. From there, we began to work together. She had a happy life and career for the most part. All she truly wanted to do was make the necessary changes to her practice that would yield more profits. We discussed her rates and the possibility of more slots. I still remember one of our first sessions. She disclosed that she was doing a LCSW exam prep group for free that she had been running for two years. She was super excited to let me know that last week she had 22 participants and that the library was about to start charging her because the group was so large. Yes, you heard that correctly, she was running a group that was too large for the FREE space and she was going to have to start paying them for something that she was offering for FREE. I asked if she thought about charging for her group? Her initial responses were, "What if people can't afford it?" "What if they stop coming?" I dug a little further with her on this to see what the passing rate for her group was over the last two years and how much money she really needed to earn for her time. We settled on what my business coach would say is a lower rate than necessary.

Those who know Dee Dee know how hard it was for her to even think about this. She moved forward with charging even less than that for the group. Although she was nervous, uncertain and afraid of what it would do to those that she was helping, she did it. Guess what? They paid. I knew that this could be a really good opportunity to make this thing official as a business and not just a hobby. After some in-depth discussions and me intent on her not backing out because, "She doesn't like to ask people for money," Test Prep Central, LLC was birthed.

Fast forward over six months later, the hobby that started in her living room has now become another stream of income, her actual business and a little slice of the social work hustle. The gems that are dropped in this book are from personal experience, hard work and many tears shed. I hope that it blesses your spirit and motivates you to get out and do something you never dreamed because there are so many things you can do with your degree than they teach you in school.

The message and purpose of this book can be implemented across disciplines as social workers, marriage and family therapists, mental health counselors, case managers and others in the human services field. You can benefit from knowing you are not alone. Your desire to help others is very important and there are ways to do that and still make a decent living. As someone who's been in the helping field for over 17 years in various capacities, I can also say that more inclusion, collaboration and education on the various disciplines and how they differ and are the same lends to a more cohesive and productive world of professional helpers. Together we are a force to be reckoned with and our voices are heard louder in symphony than alone.

As the character Diamond said in the movie The Players Club, "Make the money. Don't let it make you!" The days of having three and four jobs neglecting you, your children and family is not the only path to go. I also understand that entrepreneurship is not for the faint or weak at heart either. So choosing what you want to do, how you want to do it and coming up with a plan is essential on the journey to mastering the hustle. Some may read this and think, "I'm not ready." My question to you is what do you have to do in order to get ready? How much more of you do you have to lose before you get courageous about exploring new ways to produce a better version of yourself that will enable you to do the best work of your career? We tend to be at our best when we are doing what we love, with whom we love to do it with and on our own terms. I mean, after all, that is what the social work hustle is all about.

There are two quotes that I would like to share that I feel will ignite the fire in your soul and leave you with some inspiration to at least get curious about what else is out there. The first one is by someone who's work I am trained in and I just truly admire. Dr. Brené Brown said it best, "If you're not in the arena getting your butt (ass) kicked too, I'm not interested in your feedback." It's very important to make sure you have a support system, team, business coach and/ or mentor, or minimally a business bestie that will hold you accountable and keep you on the path to your goals and help you grow your vision. The other quote I'd like to leave you with is, "Your passion and your purpose should yield profits," by yours truly. What this means is follow your dreams, the things that make you light up and feel fulfilled. The reasons you were placed on this earth oftentimes line up with what you are doing for a living. This can be a real blessing when you also give yourself permission to make it count in the profits arena. After all, this is a business and the goal is to help others and continue to be change agents. Do so by making moves and not excuses. Choose courage over fear. As a matter of fact fuck fear and do it scared! You got this!

Chasity Chandler, LMHC, MCAP, ICADC, CST, CDWF
Licensed Mental Health Counselor & Qualified MHC Supervisor
Authenticity Coach for Professional Helpers

CHAPTER ONE

OH *Hell* NAW!

Dhaima Chin, LCSW

"Even at your lowest, you're stronger than you think."
-Dhaima Chin, LCSW

On May 2011, I sat on the edge of my bed contemplating my next move. This was the moment I had been waiting for and I finally made it. I was overly excited. For me, this milestone in my life was a major accomplishment and I felt that I should have been feeling every ounce of pride in addition to happiness, joyfulness and gratefulness. However, I felt scared, anxious and worried about what my next step will be. You see, I was the first person in my family to receive my master's degree. Hell, I was the first person in my family to receive any type of degree.

My parents were both immigrants from Jamaica who came to the United States in hopes of living the American dream. They were hard workers who worked their asses off to provide for my sister and I. My mother was a beautician. She worked day and night standing on her feet. My dad on the other hand was a struggling musician. I decided when I was a young girl that I wanted to show them how much I appreciated them for all of their hard work. I decided to chase my dreams and accomplish my goals. Well, Mom and

Dad, WE MADE IT! THIS DEGREE IS OUR DEGREE!

(Note to the reader: In order for this to be an effective tool, I'm going to need you to use your imagination)!

Six years prior to 2011, I was working in the Guardian Ad Litem program as a Paralegal. The Guardian Ad Litem program is the voice for children that have been abused, neglected or abandoned. The Guardian Ad Litem is a person the court appoints to investigate which solutions would be in the "best interests of a child." I learned a lot working at this agency and I saw things differently.

I encountered several cases that involved sexual abuse, domestic violence, homelessness and education disparities. It was an eye-opener for me to see little children experiencing these hardships. I never had to worry about anything when I was a child. Though these cases were heartbreaking and devastating for me, I am grateful that I had this opportunity to experience this because it made me want to make a difference in my community. It was at that time that a co-worker of mine who told me that I should go to school and get my master's degree in social work. She told me that I had a natural talent when it came to helping others that would propel me in the social work field. I thought she was crazy to say the least. I had already gone to school and received three degrees. As far as I knew it, the Paralegal life was it for me. I was content.

A couple of days later, I encountered a case that literally changed my life forever. This was a case involving a family that was torn apart by an incident that had occurred. In summary, the case involved a father of four who had previously been gunned by unknown assailants. The mother became the sole provider for her family in what seemed like overnight. Unable to properly provide for her children efficiently, she decided to seek employment sources illegally. The mother ended up selling drugs to provide for her children. Unfortunately, her bad decision left her with a prison sentence, and the removal of her kids. Subsequently, there was no family that wanted to take in the children. Therefore, the children were placed in foster care, and was sent to live in separate homes. This was heartbreaking to me to see the children separated. I could not imagine me and my sister being separated. This case affected me because it hit so close to home and it dealt with my own African-American culture. In my culture, the things that were involved in that particular case were unheard of. Family comes first. My eyes opened and I learned that every culture deals with tragedy differently.

It was after encountering this case that it dawned on me. I was content as a paralegal, but I was not reaching my full potential. It was at that moment I decided that I was going back to school for the fourth time. I was going to be a **Social Worker**! This was my **AHA** moment. **Imagine**: Wonder Woman standing on the tallest building in her signature pose, and a light bulb over her head. That was the moment I was in, and I knew I was destined for bigger things in life.

Welcome Back...

I was once again a student in college. I don't know if it was the fact that I had gotten older, was older than most other students, or if it was just that the school environment changed so drastically since I last attended college. It was a struggle for me when I first started and I won't lie about wanting to quit. I felt overwhelmed and I couldn't keep up with the pace. One subject I struggled with before in college was math. OMG! It was my arch nemesis and I hated it with all of my might. I wasn't ecstatic about taking a math course, and I thought that I would push it off as long as I possibly could. My plan was a complete bust. I was assigned a math course the first semester. Fuck! By this time, I really felt heartbroken. I couldn't believe that this one class was going to stop me from achieving my dreams of being a social worker. Why the hell was this happening to me?

I sat in the front of the class, attended all the classes and somehow I still didn't understand what the hell was going on. It's like they were speaking in ancient alien hieroglyphics. I was so lost. During that whole semester, I kept telling myself…keep pushing, you can do it. Then my other self would tell me hell nawww you don't have this! Stop while you're ahead!

I became so desperate that I started asking anyone in the class for help. I watched all the students who raised their hands to answer all the professor's questions. That's when I noticed Nadia. I approached Nadia and told her that I was struggling in the class, and she said so confidently, "This class is easy!" To this day, I wonder if we were in the same class. Nadia helped me tremendously and I was able to pass.

At the same time, I remember I had to write a paper in APA style in another class. All I could think is, "WTF is APA style?" Still to this day, I don't know what it is, but you didn't hear that from me. Ok, moving forward with the story, I turned my paper in and I knew at best it was a B paper. Ha!

The professor showed my ass what letter grade my paper was. Can you believe she gave me a whole, "F?" Like seriously, what the fuck?

I was fuming that day. After class, I walked over to the professor and politely asked her, "Why did I get an F?" She told me, "You didn't follow directions," and proceeded to tell me about the APA formatting.

It just so happened that along this journey on that day, I met one of the coolest women I know. That was the day I met Sasha. It was by chance that she was still in that class that day and wanted to talk to the professor herself. When she was done talking to the professor, she came over to me and told me that she would help me fix my paper. I ended up getting a "B" after Sasha's help. She became one of the leading supporters in my educational journey.

She helped me with studying, was my accountability partner and someone I could talk and vent to about this crazy journey. Needless to say, without Sasha, I wouldn't be where I am today. It was a long two years, but I made it through the storm. I learned a lot, and made plenty of sacrifices along the way.

For instance, many people don't know this about me, but I was a bartender for those four years in college. I wasn't able to work a full-time job because I was attending school full-time and I had my internship that needed to be completed. I was ready to see what was on the other side. As a bartender, I learned many things. I learned the importance of networking, customer service and empathy. I also learned the importance of being present with every customer. I learned how to put my issues aside and still smile. These are important skills that are used repeatedly in the social work field.

Have you ever heard the expression, "Closed mouths don't get fed?" Well I wanted to eat! **MESSAGE:** You have to network. It's not what you know, it's who you know.

Commencement Day...

I sat there anxiously through the program and the time came for me to walk across that stage to get the paper that I worked so hard for. Finally, the moment came for us to form a line. They began calling the names in alphabetical order. Then finally I heard, Dhaima Chin! I inhaled and dashed quickly across that bitch to get my degree. I posed with the President of the school, took a couple more pictures after I exited the stage and I was ready to celebrate.

I had a new lease on life and the very next day I started looking for a J-O-B. It was such an exhilarating feeling to search for the type of work that I had a passion for and that I worked so hard towards. Nothing could stop this feeling that I was experiencing, except one thing,

I COULDN'T FIND A FUCKING JOB!

Two months later, I was still unemployed. There were literally no jobs in sight and I couldn't have been more FLUSTRATED, (that's a combination of flustered and frustrated). I was pissed, angry and unemployed! When I say all types of shit ran through my mind, they really did. Why didn't anyone tell me this shit could happen before I graduated? Why did I have to find out the hard way? Was this happening to other fresh social workers? When will it end? Most importantly, why was this happening to me?

I was sending resumes out continuously and no one was calling me back. I started to believe I was going to be a bartender for the rest of my life. But still I didn't give up. I took an impromptu trip to Orlando one day and while I was there, I applied for at least a dozen jobs. Hell, I figured it wouldn't hurt to apply, I was open to relocating at this moment.

Maybe a week after applying to all these jobs, three of them called me back and offered me an interview. So inside I'm screaming YESSS! Now I just have to sell myself to the employers. I went to all three interviews with a promise that I would hear back from them by the end of the week. I experienced mixed feelings about the promises I heard because this wasn't my first job. I've heard these things before and never received a call back. On the other hand, I was happy because I got a reply, went on the interview and was promised a call back.

I was literally driving back home from Orlando, when I received an unexpected phone call. It was after that call I immediately felt all my fears were pushed aside. I was so overwhelmed with joy that I had to pull over and take it all in. Between my shouts and praises to God, I quickly realized that I had made it. In as little as three weeks, I started my new career as a Social Worker. What could be better than that... right?!

MESSAGE: When sending resumes to different jobs, use keywords from the job description to stand out more. Read and dissect the job's description, edit your resume to highlight your skills and experiences that apply. Don't forget to write thank you letters after the interview.

Reflections I will say that the beginning of this journey seemed hard and damn near impossible at times. However, once you make up your mind to pursue this career, you should stick to it. It's not always going to be a smooth ride, in fact you will encounter many bumps in the road. Sometimes in life, you need to make sacrifices along the way.

Questions

1. Why do you want to become a social worker? Or why did you become a social worker?
2. Do you have a Nadia or a Sasha around you?
3. When was the last networking event you attended?
4. When is the next networking event you're attending?
5. When was the last time you reviewed your resume?
6. Do you role-play interview with friends and colleagues in order to be better prepared?

Notes

_____

_____

_____

_____

_____

_____

CHAPTER 2

Oh Shit! WHAT'S NEXT?

Fuck what you feel, think about what's real!

I remember my first day as a social worker as if it was yesterday. I was so eager to jump in to the field. I was shadowed by a seasoned social worker for nearly a month. I couldn't wait for her to leave my side because I was ready to do this on my own. Boy were those the easy days. I soon would learn that there is no such thing as easy in social work.

This was my chance to show what I learned in all my training and education. I was going to take the skills that I learned and apply them to each and every situation that was presented to me. I was going to use those book lessons and make them work for me.

If I could go back and tell my young social work career something, it would probably be to sit your ass down. Even though all the things you learn in class are familiar, it's very different when applying them to the real world.

While I was at that job, I saw some things that I couldn't believe. I've been yelled at and called out my name. There was this one incident that I will never forget. I had to attend a court hearing early that morning. Generally, when I have court hearings, I dressed in, "court attire." Sometimes, I would wear black slacks and a blouse with a blazer and my comfortable church heels. This particular day, I switched it up and decided to wear a skirt, which was below my knees. After the hearing, I had to visit the parents on my caseload. When I got to the house the father opened the door and I started the visit with him. Well this didn't sit well with the mother as she called me a, "bitch," homewrecker and deceitful."

She accused me of trying to steal her boyfriend away from her and that I was trying to seduce him by wearing a short skirt. Whoa...what the fuck?! I didn't sign up for this shit. I left their home, went directly to the office and told my supervisor what happened. I typed my notes in the computer. The mother called the office to file a complaint against me.

MESSAGE: Be mindful that people have other issues going on. Don't match their energy and don't take things personal.

First Paycheck

I compared my check with money I made previously as a bartender. I was making twice as much then, than what I made in two weeks here. WTF! I had my master's degree.

This was certainly not the pay range the professors spoke of when I was working to obtain my degree. I wanted to know what was going on and why I feel as if I had been deceived?

I quickly started weighing the pros and cons. Even though I was getting a mileage check, it was not enough to cover the expenses and wear and tear I was putting on my car. I had to get gas, tune-ups and tires more frequently because 90% of my work was driving. In under a year, I had added close to 100,000 miles on my car.

It's not hard to understand why people do some of the things they do like scamming or selling drugs. I mean for a master's degree, all I had to show for it was a badge, an old ass laptop and a Blackberry phone that had buttons. This was not what I imagined while I was sitting in my graduate classes or praying that I found a job in the social work field. However, as time passed working at this agency it had gotten a little better. I learned how to use that old ass laptop, I got familiar with using that Blackberry answering all my client calls and checking on them daily. I learned how to improve my time management skills, writing and communication skills. This was helpful in the field then and it's helpful in the field now. I found myself connecting with clients and enjoying my work even more. I realized that I enjoyed my job more because I had clients I could relate to and actually help. This progress made me feel like a real social worker. However, I could not stop wondering if I had made the right decision. Maybe I should have stayed a bartender, or in Miami. I thought I could really make a living doing this? Could I find another job? Is Social Work really for me?

A little background about my first job.

I worked in the child welfare system because I received a stipend, which was very beneficial.

MESSAGE: Stipend students will have access to faculty mentors with extensive child welfare experience who are hired to work specifically with them. The goal of the Title IV-E program is to create and support a professional workforce in child welfare for the state of Florida. Eligible students will receive a $6,000 stipend per year for up to two years. Part-time graduate students will receive $4,000 per year for up to three years.

At this time, I decided that I did enjoy the job. However, I wanted more and I would obtain it by getting my license as a clinical social worker. When I was in school, I never thought that I would ever get my license. After seeing how child welfare worked, I quickly changed my mind. I saw that being a clinician would give me one-on-one interaction with the clients to help them resolve issues that they were going through.

The next process was to complete my application for the registered clinical intern license. When filling out this application, I learned that I needed a clinical supervisor. I wish there was a supervisory support network when I was looking for a supervisor to help me choose an appropriate supervisor.

MESSAGE: When picking a supervisor, here are some things to consider:

1. Try to find a well-diversified supervisor that shares the same interests as you.
2. Research and ask questions.
3. Learn the supervisor's style or theoretical approach.
4. Find a supervisor that you feel comfortable with. It doesn't make sense to find a supervisor that you can't stand or don't like.
5. Do some research on prices supervisors charge. Higher

prices doesn't always equal more quality supervision. The goal is to find an experienced supervisor who can help you better understand the field of social work.

6. Invest in yourself by taking specialized training to sharpen your, "niche."
7. Understand you will be working toward being a well rounded clincan.
8. Be committed to the cause and the purpose.
9. The ultimate goal is to find your very own niche or specialty.
10. Your supervisor is not your therapist. If you need a therapist, find one. Don't cross boundaries.

Note to Self: Once you obtain your degree, learning is just the beginning. Make sure to keep the knives in your toolbox sharp. Therefore make certain that you are doing the best in becoming the best Social Worker by doing the work. You can achieve these things by getting CEU's, training and consulting with professionals. This is why supervision is an important step in the learning process.

Reflections

Sometimes you need to push thru your shit, in order to make your dreams happen. Make clear and precise goals.

Give your goals a start and an end date. Make some moves. Do what you need to do. The only thing that can stop you is yourself. It's time that you believe in you and don't let anything or anyone change your mind. You must have self discipline.

Questions:

1. What matters to you? (You need to see it to believe it – Make a vision board)
2. Are your dreams really worth the headaches?
3. How will you rule your destiny?
4. What does investing in yourself mean?
5. How committed are you to your goal?

Notes

_____

_____

_____

_____

_____

_____

CHAPTER 3

WTF?

"Babies fall a million times before finally learning how to walk." – Ahmir Young

So obviously this chapter is a, "What The Fuck," chapter. After I successfully registered for the LCSW exam, I finally received the registered clinical intern license. Now it was officially time for me to take the next step, and that was to take the test! I was ready, I was still full of book knowledge mixed with some real-life experiences. I prepared the day before my test by going over some old study materials. I was like, "Boom, I got that answer right, and boom I got that answer right!" All I had to do was carry the same confidence into the test.

I got up that morning, took a shower and made a hearty, but healthy, breakfast. I was super excited, and I remember having a spring in my step that day. I jumped into my car, crunk up my trap music and headed to the testing site. I planned my time carefully, and roughly four hours later, I would be walking out that same test site with a passing score. I made it to the test site, signed in, was given a locker to place my belongings and I sat at the desk I would stay for the duration of the test.

Time to take the test...

Question 1... WTF is this??

.

.

.

Question 80...did they give me the wrong test?

.

.

.

Question 170...Seriously what the fuck is this?

When I submitted the test a three-minute survey popped up. I was still excited about seeing my passing score, so I completed the survey and soon as I entered the last part, my test scores popped up.

FAIL

What the fuck? How is that possible? I was certain that I got most of the answers right. Right? The first thing I did was look over the scores. Now I know some of y'all can relate to this feeling. I felt like that test miscalculated my scores. How could I get the most wrong in an area that I was so fluent in? Ethics! I use ethics every day. I mean I'm the most ethical person I can think of, but apparently that test thought differently. My mindset and knowledge on ethics did not match the ethics questions on that damn test. I felt lost, almost like I did not know what I was doing.

I was devastated, and even more embarrassed. I had told everybody and their mommas that I was taking the test that weekend. As soon as I collected my belongings and turned my phone on, it wouldn't stop buzzing. I was getting back-to-back calls and text messages. Everybody wanted to hear from the person that went in to take that test, but the person who came out didn't want to talk to anyone. I found myself turning off my phone for the entire weekend. I was only answering my work phone and only a select few had that number.

I couldn't wrap my mind around the fact that I failed the test. It was unbelievable because I knew this stuff. I couldn't figure out where I went wrong. I felt incompetent after taking the test. The test defeated me, it took my life, my hopes and my dreams. Failing this test was very detrimental to me. It took some time for me to refocus and figure out what my next step would be.

Every social worker that I was around was content about

where they worked, nobody wanted to change and elevate. Before I was ready to elevate and change, afterwards I fell in sync with them. I continued to do the supervision hours, I put the test to the side and moved the books away from me, I took a hiatus. I was torn between pursuing social work and fighting harder for it. I was even thinking about just walking away from social work because I could make more money doing something else, (anything else).

Months later, I found an online MeetUp study group. I met Lisa in the very first meeting I attended. We hit it off. She was doing all the things I wanted to do before I failed the test. She was preparing for her test, and she was one of the first people that I ran into that was dedicated to elevating. That encouraged me so much. I decided to go back and re-take my LCSW exam. I knew this license was going to open doors for me and I wanted to brace myself for it. I always kept that in the back of my mind. Over the course of preparation for the exam, I talked to Lisa several times on the phone and in person. During that time, Lisa had passed her exam and I knew for sure that I was making the right decision by re-engaging in the exam prep.

Fast forward maybe nine months later, I was ready to

take the exam again. I studied the entire week before the exam. The day before the exam, I went to the salon and got a massage. I was relaxed and ready to go. I jumped into my car, cranked up my trap music and headed to the testing site. I planned my time carefully, and in roughly four hours, I would be walking out that same test site with a passing score.

Test Results:

FAIL

Not a-fucking-gain! Surely, I thought these results were wrong. I couldn't wait to see my results and where I fucked up at. I studied too hard to fail this test. But wait, I noticed there was a huge difference in my previous score. I had failed by 10 points this go round. I was back in that place that I was in before. I felt like this license was a lifeline for me. I felt like all my hopes and dreams were flushed down the toilet. Something had to change and I had to be the one to change it.

I opted for a change in my environment and decided to move back to Miami. I changed my supervisor as well. I got to the point where I thought about re-taking the test. I was still talking to Lisa and she provided support for me when I needed it. I gave up any type of life that I had outside of work. I dedicated my extra time to studying and I studied hard. Nearly a year later, I signed up for the test again.

By now you should know the pattern.

FAIL

I failed the test by three points. AHHHHHH! All these materials and studying I did, was still not enough. I talked to others who had successfully passed the test, I researched and nothing happened. It seemed that nobody around me cared that I failed. I can't tell you have many times I heard, "It'll be ok," or, "It's just a test." It wasn't just a test to me. It was so much more than that. This test was my life! I knew that this test was a significant key to my success. It was so close, but so far at the same damn time. How could I get these people to see that it was more than just a test? My sharing circle had decreased significantly. Maybe three people knew that I was taking this test. I was back in that space again, with this exam lingering over my head taunting me.

That was strike three and I was out!

Hold up this ain't no damn baseball!

Remember, a baby falls a million times before they walk.

At the same time as me failing my test, there was a change in management at my job. The supervisor at work was so laid back and understanding of the duties of a child welfare worker. I was so happy and satisfied working under him. It was wonderful and there were never any issues.

One day, he gets a call from another agency and he suddenly left, there was a new sheriff in town. OMG! She was such a dictator, which means she was a bitch. She was new, therefore she had to prove herself to the agency. She micro managed every minute of the hours, which was so fucking annoying. This is when I knew I had to leave, in other words, I had to PASS my test.

MESSAGE: Sometimes the universe has to make you uncomfortable to make you push yourself out of your comfort zone. Therefore push yourself because no one else is going to do it for you.

Reflections

1. Has there ever been a time in your life where you thought you were a failure?
2. Have you ever felt like giving up?
3. What have you done to keep from giving up?

4. What are some stress relieving methods you think can be beneficial to you while preparing for the test?

Notes

_____

_____

_____

_____

_____

_____

CHAPTER 4

YOU *Got* THIS!

Sometimes the fear doesn't go away so you have to do the damn thing afraid!

I found myself experiencing those same mixed feelings as before and I didn't like that shit at all. I knew something else had to change on top of all the changes I had already made. But what could I do differently? What was I willing to do differently? Regardless of how I felt, I knew that I was going to take this test again. I was not going to let it defeat me. I was NOT going to be this test's bitch! I was destined for bigger things damnit!

So, I became even more strict on myself.

When I came in from work on the weekends I studied until it was time to go to bed. Weekends…ha! I didn't know what those were anymore. I literally became a hermit and I camped out in my room behind closed doors away from my family and I studied. I studied, and studied and studied. I took practice tests that were four hours long that I thought simulated the exam. I researched different test-taking methods.

I researched the methods I felt would help lower my anxiety. I researched planning, and so I got a planner and planned out every day and what time I would commit to studying. I researched oils and lotions. I learned certain oils had essential components in them that would help me to relax and stay calm. I recited positive affirmations daily. "I will PASS this test." It was one thing to recite it, but you better believe it. You know the Bible says, "Faith without works is dead, so I kept the faith and studied daily. I researched more calming techniques that I thought would help me and stumbled upon a method called tapping.

Tapping is a method that's thought to restore energy balance by providing relaxation and anxiety relief. Tapping was, and still is, useful for me. It helped me to relax, focus a little better and lower my anxiety. The last thing I researched was breathing methods. Sometimes it can be something that's small, overlooked, and so simple, and at the same time be the most effective tool you can use. I've been breathing my whole life, so it wasn't that hard to master. When I found myself feeling frustrated, I just took a second to breathe which allowed me to refocus and gain control over my anxiety.

I continued to do my supervision hours, and during this time, I talked to my supervisor about my concerns. My supervisor was very encouraging and she offered support whenever I called her. She taught me how to lower my anxiety, and how it played a big part in my test taking. She gave me hope. And of course I prayed.

My supervisor gave me one important piece of advice that still sticks with me today. She recommended that I write my name followed by the LCSW title one hundred times on paper. It looked something like this:

Dhaima Chin, LCSW

MESSAGE: Do you see what I did there?

Looking at my name with the title that I had been trying to acquire was a motivational push for me. I was more determined than ever to take this test again. I will admit that this was an enlightening period for me. I learned how to master so many tools in the process. The #1 tool I utilized was a planner which helped me to keep track of each topic of the exam. Once I conquered one subject, I moved on to the next before you knew it, I was done. These are tools that I was going to use when I faced this exam again.

Tools
1. Planner

2. Relaxation Techniques
3. Visualization (Affirmations)
4. Effective Studying Techniques

Having a support team is also important and extremely helpful. My support system knew I was studying for the exam, but only one person knew I was re-taking the exam. I only told my best friend; Angel. Every conversation that Angel and I had revolved around taking the test and passing it. I know she must've gotten tired of me talking about this test and volunteering her time to help me study. She was an instrumental part in my preparation. She would sit for hours with me, reading questions and rationales. She showed sheer dedication to the cause and I thank her for that.

Ninety-one days later...I was sitting at that table in front of a computer.

This was the moment when I was going to find out what I was made of and how I was going to implement all the tools I had learned. For some reason I was less anxious this go round, so those tools were working. The questions were in English, and they all looked familiar, that was a plus. I went to the restroom at least four times not to use it, but to wash my hands and help me refocus. This definitely helped lower my anxiety. I learned that this exam was not a sprint, it was a marathon. I had conditioned myself for this exam, and it seemed to be working for the best.

I had gotten to the point where I had to click the submit button. Suddenly, my anxiety kicked back in and in my mind I was trying to calm myself down off the ledge.

AHHH…relax…YOU GOT THIS! Maybe I should go back and recheck all my answers. BREATHE. You don't have time to check all these. Think about the ones you think you might have wrong. BREATHE. You know this shit. You worked so hard for this. Don't second guess yourself. This is your time…your moment. WOMAN THE FUCK UP! BREATHE!

CLICK

We would like for you to participate in a brief three minute survey:
CLICK. CLICK. CLICK. CLICK. CLICK. CLICK. CLICK.

Thank you for your time!

PASS

YESSSSSSSSSSSSSSSSSSSSSSSS! I finally defeated this test. I felt such a relief, almost like a weight lifted off of me. I was so happy and shocked at the same time. I was trembling walking from the site all the way to my car. When I got in the car, I let out one of the loudest screams that I have ever belted from my mouth. I couldn't believe that I passed the exam…I finally passed. This was a hurdle I thought I would never jump over.

I was extremely excited, and after I started to calm down a little, I immediately called my sister Danielle. She was happy for me, and the first thing she asked was, "Why didn't you tell me or Mommy?" I explained to her that I didn't want anyone to know that I took the test for safety measures. I told her that it was something I had to go through on my own. After I finished yelling and screaming with my sister with excitement, I hung up the phone.

I started to reflect and for the first time I realized how important lowering anxiety really is when it comes to life-changing moments like this one. There were a few things that helped me along the way. I got into a habit of using an app on my phone that was specifically for the LCSW exam. I literally used the Pocketprep app wherever I was. If I was at work taking a break, I was using this app. If I was at home in the bathroom, I was using this app. If I was sitting in the passenger seat during a car ride, I was using this app. It was convenient and it offered so many learning tools. I curbed Facebook and Instagram for this app, and everyone knows how I am when it comes to Facebook. I am a Facebook Junkie.

MESSAGE: It's important that you understand that you have to put in the time and hard work. Sacrifices will have to be made when you want to achieve something that's life changing. Utilize good study materials when you are prepping. Remember all study materials aren't effective! Some may not go into depth and deliver the substance you need to understand the logic behind the subject. Some study materials may be outdated.

Here's what to look for in good study materials:

1. Descriptive questions that explain a scenario.
2. Look for solutions or rationales that tell you the reason why an answer is the best choice or the worst

choice is.

3. Find materials from reputable companies.

Another useful tip is to find a study group. The support you receive in a study group is very effective. You want to find like minded people as yourself that's on the same vibration as you. Humans have the capability of remembering something they read, but to have a discussion about a topic is more effective implanting the memory in your brain ...***and yes that was all the MESSAGE!***

Reflections

Never give up on your dreams, and if you fail, lose, or fuck up, get up and try again. Remember Miami wasn't built in a day. I don't know how long it took to build it, but the point is it took time. So with that being said, prepare yourself for the long haul. Just do it!

1. What goals do you have?
2. What are your affirmations?
3. What steps are you taking to reach your goals?
4. How bad do you want to reach your goals?

Notes

_____

_____

_____

_____

_____

_____

CHAPTER 5

THIS *Can't* BE RIGHT!

"The truth will always be the truth, even if no one believes it." -Nipsey Hussle

Dhaima Chin, LCSW

This was it, I had officially arrived. Once I obtained my license and had it in hand, I sent it directly to HR. A few days later, HR sent my ass a letter that rocked me to my core. They told me in a nutshell, that I will get a raise, but it only equaled up to about a two dollar increase per check. What the fuck? This can't be right! I mean the exam cost more than the increase they were giving me a year.

I decided at that time that it was time to look for another job. This was a hard decision for me because I really loved my job and I loved working with that population. But I knew that I was worth more than they were willing to pay. So the job search began. I was looking for something that equaled my worth. It was such an amazing feeling to be looking for a position as an LCSW. There were so many opportunities available, and I had the pleasure of finding a job that was in the scope of my specialty.

One of my close friends is an LCSW and she loves her

job. She worked at a dialysis clinic and stated that she would be happy to give my resume to her supervisor. After I visited the center to drop off my resume, I realized that I did not want to work in that type of environment. **MESSAGE:** Do some research about the job. Go in person and not just online. Sometimes you have to get a feel for the environment.

When I started working as a social worker supervisor I was making $50,000 a year. You couldn't tell me nothing! I was sitting on top of the world. I had no prior experience as a supervisor, and the license allowed me to turn the key and open that door for opportunity. I thought working at the hospital was my dream job. It seemed like so much money because I never made that much money before. But one thing I've learned in life is you don't know until you know. Sometimes you find yourself accepting jobs that aren't a good fit for you or your specialty, "niche." Tread lightly in this area. Always be mindful of what you know you can do and your limitations. Stay in your lane. The question you need to ask yourself is how you will be a positive asset to a company. I had to learn that your mindset, motivation, attitude, network, all depends on your finances. **You are your most valuable asset.**

For the meantime, I was happy, stable and learning a lot every day.

MESSAGE: Before you accept a job offer, check out the salary. I was so happy for a new opportunity that I did not negotiate the pay. After I got settled in and talked to other supervisor's that worked for different hospitals, I learned that they were making $60,000 to $70,000 a year. I say that to say this; don't be afraid to ask for what you are worth, the most they can say is, "No."

Around the same time I stepped into my new career, I wanted to find more social workers like myself. So I created a Meetup group for social workers online. In this group, I made so many connections. This group also led me to Shavonne and she was a founding member of another group on Facebook called South Florida Social Workers Connect.

We shared so much in common with the fact that we both wanted to meet more social workers. I soon came on board to help with the management of the group and as of now, we have close to one thousand members and growing daily.

It was also during this time that I found another group

on Facebook which completely changed my life in so many ways. I decided to join the group and I've been a member ever since. The group is a support group for therapists. I enjoyed the conversation and discussions that were shared. The group does an annual trip and I decided to go and meet some of the therapists I have been talking to online. I really didn't know any of the members of the group until I went on the trip, which by the way was to Cuba.

The trip changed my life by opening my eyes. I was able to see therapists actually living their dream and purpose. After witnessing this, I knew there had to be a change I wanted to experience. I overheard one of the therapists saying how she easily earned six figures a year. My eyes and ears lit up in curiosity. WTF? This can't be right…can it? I've never heard a social worker say anything close to making that much a year. I've heard other professions like doctors, rappers, dancers, models and even Instagram socialites make that much a year, but never social workers. Time to change that!

MESSAGE: She told me the secret was to open your own business. This will allow you to make as much, or as little money, you would like to make.

I'm a goal-getter! Now it was time for me to implement a plan and put it into action.

According to Psychology Today, the **imposter syndrome** is a psychological term referring to a pattern of behavior where people doubt their accomplishments and have a persistent, often internalized fear of being exposed as a fraud. This can be a crippling situation that can sneak up on you and you're not always aware of it. In order to prevent imposter syndrome, you need to change your mindset. The goal is to become the best at your 'niche" (Brand Yourself) so, you must decide how you want to be known as in the Social Worker community. You must become fearless, accept truth, accept constructive feedback and set reachable goals in a timely matter.

MESSAGE: If you want to stop feeling like an imposter stop thinking like an imposter.

Reflections

Fuck fear... use your faith and intuition. Write your own destiny. Create your own path. Trust your energy. You're in the right place at the right time.

1. What is your biggest fear?

2. What are you doing to overcome this fear?

3. Who can help you face this fear?

4. Do you have Imposter Syndrome?

Notes

_____

_____

_____

_____

_____

_____

CHAPTER 6

Thrive

Money, Impact, Give Back

Everything in your past prepares you for your fucking future, it's time to move to the next chapter.

Crash course in starting a business

Naturally after hearing about this untapped income, I decided that it was time to write the next chapter in my life. I reached out to all of my mentors, and I'll admit that I was scared to take the plunge. However, when the right energy comes around, the wrong energy gets nervous. I made a plan and it was time to execute it. I took time out to write a business plan.

MESSAGE: *Pay close attention to these steps. Right now Google should be your best friend. Don't be afraid to use it.*

1. I did some soul searching to realize what my "niche" was. **MESSAGE:** This is one of the main goals you need to figure out in order to know the population you will be serving. Remember you want to brand yourself!
2. I opened my own limited liability company and named it Miami Gardens Counseling Services, LLC.

3. I didn't want Uncle Sam lurking, so I obtained an EIN number. (An employer identification number (EIN) is a nine-digit number assigned by the IRS. It's used to identify the tax accounts of employers and certain others who have no employees).

4. I opened my Business Bank Account. (Try to separate your personal money from your business money. Also, this will help later on for your business credit line.)

5. I obtained malpractice/liability insurance.

6. I acquired an NPI number. (National Provider Identifier (NPI) is a unique 10-digit identification number issued to health care providers in the United States by the Centers for Medicare and Medicaid Services.)

7. I obtained a business phone number. (It is highly recommended that you use a separate line for personal and business use. Also, make sure HIPAA compliant when using internet and fax)

8. I found a practice location. **MESSAGE**: Subleases is preferred for newbies because it is more manageable for your pockets.

9. I obtained a CAQH credentialing. The Council for Affordable Quality Healthcare (CAQH) is a not-for-

profit collaborative alliance of the nation's leading health plans and networks.

10. I joined a peer support group, which will come in handy for referrals and encouragement when times get hard.

11. I made a profile on Psychology Today. (You know that old saying, "A picture is worth a thousand words?" When you create your profile, a professional picture is strongly suggested).

12. Determine whether you want to have electronic records or paper records. (You want to make sure you secure your clients records. Remember you must keep your client's records for seven years.)

Before I knew it, everything was up and running and it didn't take long to get it started. I also had a logo created and then I made business cards for my practice. It helps to use your headshots on the business cards as its more memorable to possible contacts. One of the final steps that was executed in my business plan was creating a website. If you are a more technical savvy person, you might be able to create a website on your own, but beware that creating a website from scratch or with the help of those assisted websites can be challenging. Other solutions would be to do some research and find companies that created websites with your specifics and preferences in mind, and also keep up with the monthly maintenance of the website. After I got all that situated, I needed to attract traffic to my practice. **MESSAGE:** Networking is an important step in building a practice. It was through networking that I was able to find a reputable company that helped me create my web page, and also maintain it for me. If you have some knowledge of creating websites on your own, you can do it for free. Warning…it's hard doing it yourself if you have no formal knowledge. It is also helpful to apply for private insurance companies, or EAP's. (An employee assistance program is an employee benefit program that assists employees with personal problems and/or work-related problems that may impact their job performance, health, mental and emotional well-being.) Note: this can be time consuming. Don't worry if you are not accepted by health insurances. You can write an appeal letter to the company, to try your chances again. Other than use of insurance plans, I've learned that many clients prefer paying cash, and at least 90% of my current clients are paying with cash. **MESSAGE**: Don't be afraid to charge your clients, you are worth the pay. And please remember to get that money before you start every session unless in crisis.

One component to my private practice is supervision. If you have your LCSW for more than two years and you take a qualified supervisor course you can become a Qualified Licensed Clinical Social Worker in Florida. (Please check with your state requirements). You can become one of the gatekeepers of Social Workers. I actually love supervision. At the hospital, it was apart of my job description which I enjoyed.

As a supervisor, my experience saves the supervisee from the pitfalls that I experienced in the social work field. Supervision is a growth process where the supervisee gets a chance to ask the supervisor questions, admit errors and acknowledge struggles together. Everyday, I learn something new which is beneficial for me and my supervisee.

Helping other social workers sharpen their tools is something I absolutely live for. Therefore, I knew when I opened my private practice, I would want to specialize and monetize supervision. I love talking about a topic which is unfamiliar with a student and watching as they receive the message. I love to see their eyes light up with this newfound information.

Another component is internship. This is a part of private practice that is underutilized in the community. I feel an internship is a great part of the learning opportunity in social work. In my opinion, internships are the foundation. When a licensed practitioner partners up with schools, it's a win-win. You get a chance to teach a student something and apply their book knowledge to real world situations. Also, you get a chance to give back to the school by guiding and creating another awesome social worker in the world. **MESSAGE:** Even if you haven't gotten your license, please try to participate as a field supervisor. This will help sharpen your skills as well as the student's skills. *Field instructors are eligible to receive a tuition waiver to apply at any state school to receive six hours of free tuition to be used in one semester for *each student that you supervise for an entire internship. (Please check with your state requirements).*

MESSAGE: Social Workers that want to further their education please look into fellowship programs, this provides financial support to graduate students. Fellowships are generally merit-based internal or external awards to support a student in a full-time course of study.

Opening a business allows you to see the world differently.

You will get to enjoy several perks and advantages of being a business owner. When it comes to Miami Gardens Counseling Services, everything I do is a tax write off. A cruise trip I took to Cuba was a tax write off and I received CEU's. I had to renew my license earlier this year and that was another tax write off. The mileage on my car, the paper in my copy machine and a back to school drive to give to the community were all a tax write off for me.

Reflections

Heal, grow, and help others. Giving back is a part of life. Don't hesitate to give back and mentor someone who needs it in your community. I believe that everyone could use a helping hand. You are only as strong as your community. Get into the habit of asking yourself, "Am I planting a seed for the community, I'm trying to create?"

1. Are you open to new opportunities?
2. Are you mentoring someone?
3. What are you doing to help your community?
4. Are you thriving?

Notes

_____

_____

_____

_____

_____

_____

CHAPTER 7

Self CARE

"Almost everything will work again if you unplug it for a few minutes, including you."-Anne Lamott

In college when they talked about selfcare, they discussed things that cost money such as vacations, retreats and massages. They don't talk about making a gratitude list daily, meeting with a therapist, or something as simple as unplugging for the day. I really was enjoying myself as a new entrepreneur, doing what I love and making the money from the fruits of my labor. In the process, I began to gain weight. Some people said it could have been because of stress, and others said it's because I was happy. Then I realized I was not taking care of myself and taking care of everyone around me.

Sometimes you can get so complacent in doing things until you start neglecting yourself or you may look up and notice it's too late. Shame and guilt began to consume me and I was tired, but I did not know how to slow down. Once I realized the situation I was in and what was going on, I pushed myself to be more mindful of me. I started to change my eating patterns. I started to exercise daily, and I even started meditating. I learned that no one would take time out for me except for me. I know a lot of you are working moms, and it's hard to get breaks when you have so much on your plate. This is where you tend to use your imagination. Like I mentioned earlier, self-care is often made to seem like it involves money and lots of it, that's not entirely true. "If you unplug something and leave it for a few minutes it usually works when you plug it back up. You can stay in the comfort of your own home and practice self-care.

Self care can come in the form of physical care, emotional care, social and spiritual care. Below are some examples of different types of self care.

- You can watch a movie that you love.
- Play some loud music and dance around your house.
- Sit in your closet with the door closed and meditate for five minutes.
- Drink a glass of wine. (Do not overdo it)!
- Polish your nails.
- Brush your hair.
- Read a book or work on a puzzle.
- Turn off your phone for the day if you're able to do so.
- Go online and look at photos of whatever peaks your interest.
- Stretch, or do yoga
- Painting

- Go for a walk
- Get some sleep.
- Eat healthy foods.
- Go to a social function.
- Go to church.
- Create a support system.
- Ask for help.
- Start a journal.

In the words of Art Cathy, "I'm not going to walk around here looking like Sponge Bob." I didn't want to look like the broken down social worker like Mariah Carey portrayed in the film Precious. To notice something on your own can be hard at times. I have always heard that things catch up when you get older, and I never would have imagined receiving so many, (not so flattering), comments from a posted picture online could give me so much revelation.

Social media can be a double-edged sword. Social media drew attention to me and my private practice, but those negative comments was hurtful. Be quick to take notice to the minor changes before they become major changes.

MESSAGE: Learn to motivate people, without insulting

people. I understood that I had to start from the inside to make changes to the outside. Dr. Sebi stated, "*Eat to live, or eat to die.*" That's a very powerful message and it resonates with me because you have the power of choice. The power to choose what's good for you.

MESSAGE: Eat live food if you want to live.

Reflection

It doesn't matter what I may be going through, I still want to help others, says every social worker with a heart full of gold. With that same breath, I will tell you that you can't pour from an empty cup, so make sure your cup is filled before you start pouring. Burnout is real...avoid it at all costs!

1. What do you do for self-care?
2. What do you do to refill your cup?
3. Are you asking for help when needed?

Notes

_____

_____

_____

_____

_____

_____

CHAPTER 8

SIDE *Hustles*

A Working a 9-to-5 is good, but a side hustle is always better, especially when it's your own.

One thing I learned real quick after I received my LCSW, was I could get several side hustles. The moment I passed my LCSW test, I began helping other social workers prep to pass their exam. After all my hard work and dedication, I realized the secret formula for passing the LCSW test. When I first started my study group, it was free and I had between two to five social workers coming to my house on Tuesday and Thursday nights.

These social workers were dedicated to the two days a week schedule and it showed. They came prepared and ready to learn. At the time, I was a foster parent of four children and my home could get quite noisy at times even though, I was embarrassed, that didn't stop them because they remained engaged the entire time.

We did this for a few months, and I commended my students for showing that level of dedication through and through. As the social workers I was working with began passing their test, they started to tell other social workers about me and the study sessions they were using. MESSAGE: Word of mouth can make you and it can break you. I was happy as hell that the word around town was working in my favor, and it showcased my passion of helping and encouraging other social workers.

Before I knew it, I no longer had space at my home anymore to hold the sessions because the group size started to increase fast. Therefore, I decided to move the study group to the library which offered more space and convenience. Instead of having the sessions twice a week for an hour, I now was hosting it once a week for two hours. It was nice meeting up every Sunday morning doing something I loved, and sharing a common goal with the other attendees. I hosted these study sessions for a few months. The students started referring me to other students that wanted to pass the exam. I noticed one or two new people would attend each session and I was eager to help social workers.

Then one Sunday morning, 22 people showed up in the room at the library. It was hard to contain my excitement through the shock. My study group had more than doubled since its inception. After the session was over, the librarian came to me and told me that having more than 10 people in the room was a fire hazard. She proposed that I use another room in the library which was bigger. Sounded like a great plan, until she continued talking. She told me that in order to reserve the room every Sunday it would be $100. What the hell? That was definitely outside of my budget and out of the question. I simply couldn't afford the upgrade. MESSAGE: Beware of monkey wrenches.

Later on that day, I called and spoke with my mentor Chasity and she gave me a great idea. She suggested that I start charging for the study group to see the students dedication and commitment. She stated, "People who are financially invested are usually the ones who are mentally invested." I thought about it for a while and I said, "Fuck it, let me see what it do!"

This struck a chord with me because I felt way better when I was preparing for my exam. Also this was a prime example of the imposter syndrome. Why would they pay me? The real question is Why would they not pay me? Why did I feel I wasn't good enough to offer study services? I was allowing the imposter syndrome to take over. After careful consideration and research, I put it out there and let me tell you once I did, I was shocked and emotionally touched. It worked. I was struggling with wondering how this would affect my passion and hustle, and who would pay for my services. Everyone shocked me and was willing to pay for the class. In fact, so many people decided to pay for the classes that I had to divide the two hour classes up by doing one class on Saturday and two classes on Sunday. It seemed like a lot of work, but I truly enjoyed doing this. I have strong work ethic and I'm used to a busy schedule. As long as I'm being productive, and in this case helping others, I truly feel that it's worth it.

I LOVE teaching the LCSW study group and bringing people together. I want you to keep in mind my mentor used to always say, "By the time you realize your worth, you'll be worth much more." That's a powerful statement when you think about it. How often do you downplay or downgrade your worth? Go for what you know and show your worth.

There are several side hustles available to social workers that will allow you to use your skills and trainings. Think about seven streams of income. NOT seven jobs! You don't have to have all seven, I just want to change your mindset to the hustler inside of you. MESSAGE: Don't forget about building your credit game up. Self Lender is a credit builder account that can help you build credit and save money at the same time! Build Credit Responsibly. Withdraw Savings at End. Low Monthly Payments. Build Payment History. Establish Your Credit. My Self Lender referral code is: https://selflender.com/refer/10864473.

"If you don't find a way to make money while you sleep, you will work until you die." –Warren Buffett

1. Earned income from working at your job. (9 to 5… trading time to for money)

2. Profit income from buying and selling.(Ebay, Amazon, Poshmark)

3. Interest income from lending money. (CD, Money market account)

4. Dividend income from owning stocks. (Roth IRA)

5. Rental income from renting out property. (Real Estate)

6. Capital gains income from when assets increase in value. (buy low, sell high)

7. Royalties income from others using your work. (intellectual or creative property example: song writers)

MESSAGE: Be creative and expand your options. Don't be afraid to surround yourself with professional people such as doctors, lawyers and educators.

Here's a list of some things that you can do.

- Private practice (Collaboration)
- Sublease Office
- Speaking Engagements
- Assessments
- Private Contracts
- Guardianship (Healthcare Proxy)
- Adoption Home studies
- Investments (Real Estate and Roth IRA)
- Create an App
- Design something
- Sell something
- Buy and Resell Items (New and Used)
- CEU's Provider
- Courses, Webinars, Workbooks
- T-Shirts, Bags, Mugs
- Affiliate Income
- Adjunct Professoring (College and Online)
- Write a Book (wink wink)

MESSAGE: Residual income is a must! Everyone should

be investing in their future, whether it be Roth 401K, Roth IRA, Crypto Currency, Bitcoin, and/or Gold coins. Make it a personal goal to invest 10% of your check.

My suggestion is to open an independent Roth IRA so you can trade stocks and bonds outside of your 9 to 5 retirement account. If your 9 to 5 has a match program go ahead and join however you still want to be able to independently invest in your future. Example: If my company was matching 4% into my Roth IRA, I would put the match 4% and 6% I would put into an independent Roth IRA so I can have more control of my money and invest in whatever stock I choose too. Patience and consistency are the key. " Patience is bitter, but the reward is sweet." I find it more convenient and far more helpful when you make things automatic. When they are withdrawn automatically you don't even have to think about it coming out of your paycheck. Believe me when I say you won't miss something you never had. After, you invest in your Roth IRA make sure you enter into the "DRIP program" to reinvest your dividends. MESSAGE: Everyone is going to die eventually one day. Buy Life Insurance.

Traveling social work is something that's under-utilized in the social work field. In fact, one never really hear much about travel social work. It was never something that was brought up in college and given as an option to explore. You probably never hear your co-workers talking about it. I want to change thatI want to change your perception on these types of jobs. I want you to utilize this option as much as you can. I once met someone while I was on vacation. It turns out that he was a traveling social worker. I had an in-depth conversation with him and he gave me so much insight on his work life. He also shared that he enjoyed his line of work because he was able to help so many people, and he felt like he was always on vacation.

If you love to travel and you love social work, (and I'm sure that you do if you're reading this), travel social work would be a plus for you. Not only does it combine two passions, but it's a great learning tool to expand your knowledge and your experience. This is a list of traveling social work companies:

- Anderson Group
- Aya
- Club Staffing
- Favorites
- Focus Staffing
- Green Key
- HETEC

- Loyal Source Military Assignment's
- Maxim
- Med Options
- Med Partera
- Medical Staffing Solutions LLC
- MedPartners
- MedTravelers
- Meleeo Health Care Solutions
- National Health Care Recruiters
- Soliant (School Social Work)
- The Atlantic Group
- The Social Service Staffing
- Therapy travelers
- Tootie Tou health source global

Reflection

If you do what you love, then you never have to work a day in your life. Please pay attention to who is doing what you want to do and follow that person. I would suggest you connect with the person online or offline to pick the person's brain. You can even ask the person to become your mentor.

1. What is your side hustle? (Is it your passion?)
2. Have you learned to master it?

3. Who does it the best? (This should be your mentor).

4. What goals do you have for financial success?

5. Are you saving for your future?

6. Did you open an independent Roth IRA?

Notes

_____

_____

_____

_____

_____

_____

CHAPTER 9

BRING IT *All* TOGETHER

You should never stop learning or growing.

It was once said that the two most important days of our lives are the day we are born and the day when we discover why we were born. FIND YOURSELF! You can't help or lead others if you don't know who you are and what you're doing. You need to be a master at who you are. One of the best ways to figure out what your purpose is to do a little to a lot of soul searching.

It might not be something that comes to you right away, but in due time it will. Take all the time you need when you're looking for answers. **MESSAGE:** Don't be afraid to explore, explore, explore.

After I finish with my MSW, two careers I wish I explored were Hospice Social Worker and Long-term Insurance/ Health Care.

Things to Remember

In this field, you will learn that you can't be, "Captain Save Everybody." As a social worker, you have to let everybody evolve at their own time and at their own pace. You need to allow the universe to make that decision and understand that you can't rush the process. Stop trying to rush and evaluate the process and let the process take its place. Social workers, please take this time to enjoy the ride. It may not always be a smooth ride, but in the end you will reach your destination. I wish I had a chance to just tell myself to relax, and soak it all in. I wish I could tell the younger social worker in me that it will be okay and not to worry and stress about everything. Stress isn't good for you and it does not make any situation better or more tolerable. Just by learning and implementing small tools can make a difference. These tools can help keep you mindful, help improve your overall mood and deal more appropriately with your current situation.

Don't allow any situation to make you miss out on life, enjoy each day and every breath you take. Get comfortable and move at your own pace. It's imperative that you learn that you can't change everything because you don't have control over everything. Make self-care a part of your daily routine. Go to the beach, drink a cup of coffee, drink some wine, listen to some relaxing music, and BREATHE damnit! Let your body and mind connect, "Woosah."

Don't be afraid to think outside of the box and be different.

Don't be ashamed or feel guilty about being you…be the authentic you. It's a new day and you have a new mindset. Open your arms wide for the future and be prepared to capture it. Start to embrace your new beginnings, because there will be plenty more to come. It's okay to say, "no," sometimes you can't always say, "yes," and that's okay.

Sometimes things may become overwhelming, but guess what? You're not a robot; you're human. With that being said, it's ok to cry sometimes. It's perfectly ok to unplug yourself for a while until you are able to refocus. Show yourself that you love yourself and that you put yourself first. When you get back on track, get to grinding because regardless of all the positive affirmations or thoughts you use, life is hard and it doesn't stop. Social Worker Students: Please enjoy your time in school. Don't rush the process.

MESSAGE: Support other people and other people will support you.

Reflections:
Surround yourself with people that will hold you accountable for your bullshit and your fuck ups, but at the same time will also clap for you when you are doing well.

Make sure you create a solid tribe for yourself.

1. Who is in your tribe?
2. What is your next big project?
3. What was the most valuable thing you learned from this book?

Notes

_____

_____

_____

_____

_____

_____

Dhaima Chin, LCSW

THANK YOU!!!

I am so thankful!

Go out and Hustle Social Worker's

I want to thank you for purchasing my self-help book, I hope you are able to learn and grow in your walk in the Social Work field. I hope you can feel my enthusiasm through the pages of the book. Invest in yourself, it is the best investment you can make! Trust the process and take a lot of risks. Create positive results for you and your community. To my Friends and Family: You don't know how special each and every one of you was to me in my process of being a social worker. I want to thank all of those that helped me in my journey. Each and everyone of you played an instrumental part in who I am today, and the goals I strive for. I am forever grateful.

Peace, Love, and Social Work

Dhaima Chin, LCSW

ABOUT THE AUTHOR

Dhaima Chin is a passionate Licensed Clinical Social Worker, a Qualified Supervisor and leader who is frequently called upon for her knowledge. She is the founder of Miami Counseling Services, LLC, which provides services to patients battling mental disorder and mental illness. Dhaima is also a co-founder of Test Prep Central, where she assists other social workers who are seeking licensure with exam preparation courses.

Dhaima is an Alumni of Florida Atlantic University (FAU) and was rewarded the 2019 Alumni of the Year award. She is a member of various social associations and committees including the National Black Association of Social Workers, South Workers Social Workers Connect, Black Girls in Social Work, Black Therapist Rocks and The PAC Disability Rights Committees just to name a few.

Dhaima's goal is to motivate others, especially social

workers to extend their abilities and achieve maximum success.

You can learn more about Dhaima Chin, LCSW via:
www.miamigardenscounseling.com
FB/IG: @miamigardenscounseling

www.ingramcontent.com/pod-product-compliance
Lightning Source LLC
Chambersburg PA
CBHW032150020426
42334CB00016B/1260

9 7 8 0 5 7 8 5 5 3 1 1 5